A Product of Grace: Devotions From the Heart of a Pastor

Written by: Walter Robertson, III

Graphic Designer: Dionya F. Kelley

A Product of Grace: From the Heart of a Pastor

All scripture reference from King James Version Bible unless otherwise stated.

ISBN NO. 978-1-943409-80-8

Printed in the United States of America

Pure Thoughts Publishing LLC

www.PureThoughtsPublishing.com

Dedication

This book is dedicated to my lovely wife Latasha, to our children Akeem, La'Sha, Akeila, and to our first grandchild Stephen. To my mother Janie, and to the ones who always pushed me to write, Mother Susie and Dr. Belinda Willis, and Min. Angie Taylor-Reames (author & advisor). I love everyone of you who inspired me to be greater, and I thank God for their unfailing love, support, loyalty, dedication, and prayers.

In Memory of Walter Robertson, Jr.
(My Dad)
I am honored to carry your name.

A Product of Grace: From the Heart of a Pastor

Walter Robertson, III

Presented To

_____

By

_____

Table of Contents

A Product of Grace: From the Heart of a Pastor

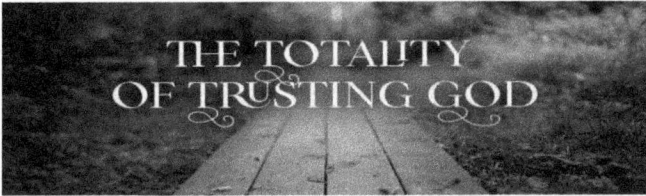

THE TOTALITY OF TRUSTING GOD

Ask yourself this question, "Have I ever doubted God?" It is likely that 100% of us would have to say yes. There are times in our lives when we will know without a doubt that God is leading or guiding us into a new direction yet we will intentionally create a delay.

I believe that our intentional delay is based upon our uncertainty. The uncertainty that will cause us to say, "I haven't been here before," or "I haven't done it like this before." If we aren't careful, this uncertainty will lead to doubt that can quickly turn into disbelief. God wants us to trust him TOTALLY! God told Abram in Genesis 12:1, "*Now the LORD had said unto Abram, Get thee out of thy country, and from thy kindred, and from thy father's house, unto a land that I will shew thee*:"

Notice, God didn't provide any details as to why, how, when, or where; He simply instructed him to go. Abram was from a family who was well-established, meaning that all of his needs were supplied based upon his earthly father. God wanted Abram to learn that in all actuality all of his needs were being supplied because of God and God alone.

Are you prepared for God to ask you to do something, or go somewhere different? Are you ready to stretch out on faith? Are you ready to separate yourself from family and friends so that you can finally hear God's purpose for your life? Are you ready to experience God in a way that you've never experienced him before? Are you ready to permit God to get up-close and personal with you? Are you ready to take God at his word concerning your life?

If you are, then let's begin to live in the words of the song "I Surrender All," by committing to Proverbs 3:5-6 "*Trust in the LORD with all thine heart; and lean not unto thine own understanding. In all thy ways acknowledge him, and he shall direct thy paths.*" Now go and remember to "TRUST GOD TOTALLY!

FAITH
VS.
FEAR

The enemy is attacking the Kingdom of God and his weapon of choice is fear. With recent attacks upon churches like vandalism, church fires, and now massacres in the church, I need to remind you to stay vigilant because this is not a new tactic that the enemy has deployed. The church has been under attack, beginning with the crucifixion of Jesus and the persecution that began soon thereafter.

The disciples ran into hiding fearing death, Christians were persecuted during the reign of Nero, and Christians to this day are persecuted in certain Muslim controlled nations simply based upon the confession of their faith. Notice this, after thousands of years of being persecuted Christians still proudly proclaim their faith in a risen savior unto this day. The bible declares in Matthew 11:12, *"And from the days of John the Baptist until now the kingdom of heaven suffereth violence, and the violent take it by force.*"

The violent are the ones who constantly find ways to form weapons and attack the people of God. A biblical example is Herod and those who worked with him to imprison John the Baptist and ultimately violently beheaded him. Their attack was easily seen since it was common knowledge based upon John's strong public rebuke of Herod. However, the enemy that the church faces in today's society is cunning and often fights from within the ranks while pretending to be Holy.

Paul spoke of them in his second letter to Timothy the third chapter verses five through seven where he says this: "*Having a form of godliness, but denying the power thereof: from such turn away. For of this sort are they which creep into houses, and lead captive silly women laden with sins, led away with divers lusts, Ever learning, and never able to come to the knowledge of the truth.*"

Be careful of these people because they know how to look like you, dress like you, and sound like you all the while they have an inward desire to cause confusion, division, and create fear among the brethren. There is at least one in every community, in every family, in every church, and on every ministry. They know that FEAR (False Evidence Appearing Real) creates doubt of what God has said resulting in faith paralysis, which is the inability to move forward because of what others may say or the possibility of failure, hurt, or pain. Will you choose to have faith or fear?

Refuse to allow your faith in God to become paralyzed by the actions, words, or deeds of those who seek to destroy in order to keep you from fulfilling your purpose. What God has ordained may be hindered, but it CAN NOT be blocked or stopped by the enemy. Remember this and be encouraged child of God, Isaiah 54:17 says, "No weapon that is formed against thee shall prosper; and every tongue that shall rise against thee in judgment thou shalt condemn. This is the heritage of the servants of the LORD, and their righteousness is of me, saith the LORD."

A pandemic has brought forth panic, isolation, and has left people wondering what to do next. People are running to grocery stores and are emptying the shelves as they stockpile and hoard essentials as they have heard that the COVID 19 virus is coming. Yet, pastors, preachers, ministers, and teachers have been declaring for years that Jesus is coming and no one is running to the churches to be saved.

It is as if our priorities have shifted to the point where we are more concerned about things that are temporal than we are about things which are eternal. Saints of God, things should not be like this. Now is a great season to witness the love of God to a world that is seeking answers and hope. Now is the time for every believer to take a stand in the midst of turmoil and panic and declare that Jesus Christ is the answer. This virus has attacked one of the pillars of our faith, "the assembling together of the saints."

Be watchful, Jesus Christ is soon to return. In the meantime, this is a call to the faithful to stand in faith instead of cowering in fear. God has not given us the spirit of fear, but the spirit of power, love, and a sound mind. So my brother and my sister, stand firm in your faith and testify of the goodness of the Lord during times such as this, while having confidence that you are under the protection of the King.

> *Finally, my brethren, be strong in the Lord and in the power of His might. Put on the whole armor of God that you may be able to stand against the wiles of the devil. For we do not wrestle against flesh and blood, but against principalities, against powers, against the rulers of the darkness of this age, against spiritual hosts of wickedness in the heavenly places. Therefore take up the whole armor of God that you may be able to withstand in the evil day, and having done all, to stand. Stand therefore, having girded your waist with truth, having put on the breastplate of righteousness, and having shod your feet with the preparation of the gospel of peace; above all, taking the shield of faith with which you will be able to*

quench all the fiery darts of the wicked one. And take the helmet of salvation, and the sword of the Spirit, which is the word of God; praying always with all prayer and supplication in the Spirit, being watchful to this end with all perseverance and supplication for all the saints. ~ Eph. 6:10-18

The Blessing of Waiting

One of the greatest struggles for any believer is waiting. Face it, no one enjoys waiting because it can be tedious and sometimes even painful. Some of the toughest times in a believer's life may have come while they were waiting to be healed, waiting to be delivered, or waiting on a situation to turn around in their favor. Yes, waiting can be tough, but there is a BLESSING IN YOUR WAITING.

At first, waiting may lead to boredom. This is where the believer must remain fervent in prayer and studying the word of God. Why? An old proverb says that, "an idle mind is the devil's workshop." A lot of people will quote this as a bible verse, but in actuality, it is just an old saying that's derived from Proverbs 16:27 The Living Bible translations.

Second, we have to deal with the struggle of being impatient, which has gotten a lot of the faithful into some tight situations for a very long time. For example, Moses got impatient and struck the rock,

King Saul got impatient and made a sacrifice without the Prophet and it cost him his kingdom, Martha was impatient with Mary as she sat at the feet of Jesus, and James and John got impatient and asked Jesus if they could call down fire from Heaven.

Third, if we don't repent from the perils of our impatience and place our problems into the hands of the Lord, then sin, rebellion, and lack of trust will be the result. If we want to grow our faith in the Lord, we must learn to trust Him with the process of waiting. Waiting is both a natural and spiritual process. The farmer plants a seed and "waits" for it to grow through "faith" that it will produce a harvest. Just like the farmer, any believer who sows a seed in faith must wait for it to produce a harvest. So sons and daughters of the Most High God, be patient and trust God. He knows exactly what He is doing. There is a blessing in waiting, and "It Shall Come to Pass."

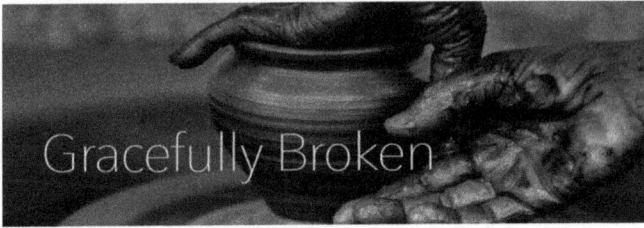

Gracefully Broken

Have you ever experienced an extremely tough situation in your life? Has it ever hurt so badly until all you could do is pray and cry? Has life ever caused you to simply lift your hands and call upon the name of the Lord?

Life has a way of putting us into situations that will break us. However, just because something is broken, doesn't mean that it doesn't still have a purpose. The potter may be creating one thing on the wheel, but after it breaks, he has the ability to reshape it into a masterpiece. I declare and decree that your brokenness will be used to usher you into your greater purpose, God's masterpiece.

When that happens and your brokenness works for your good, then you will speak differently concerning being broken. Job learned how to be *GRACEFULLY BROKEN* when he gained a deeper understanding of the grace and power of

God. Job said, "*Naked I came from my mother's womb, and naked shall I return there. The LORD gave, and the LORD has taken away; blessed be the name of the LORD,*" ~Job 1:21. Paul learned the lesson of being gracefully broken and said, "*Not that I speak in respect of want: for I have learned, in whatsoever state I am, therewith to be content,*" ~Philippians 4:11.

So let us remember that it's ok to be broken, as long as we let God's Grace use our brokenness for his glory. May the Lord give you the strength to find grace in the midst of brokenness.

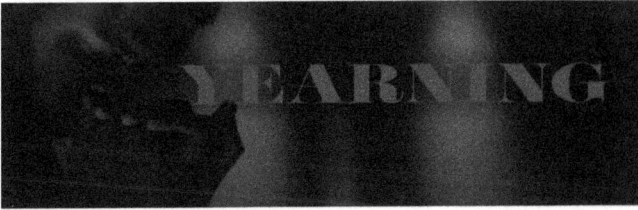

YEARNING

There was once a time where people yearned for a relationship with God that manifested through the gifts of the Spirit. Church was more than a place of membership; it was a place of worship. It is a place where those who yearned for more of God's Spirit expected Him to meet them.

As we grew in materialism, we have drifted away from the things and the presence of God. We have become satisfied with experiencing weekly glimpses of his glory, all the while yearning for more of his presence. What would happen if we thirsted for God once again more than for things?

Psalms 42:1-2 reminds us of the yearning that we must return to. It says, *"As the deer pants for streams of water, so my soul pants for you, my God. My soul thirsts for God, for the living God."*

Let us move away from materialism and make God a priority. He wants a personal relationship with you because he is a personal kind of God. Picture that, God yearns for you just as much as you yearn for him. So let us all return to our first love.

Have you ever felt as if your back was against the wall and there was no way out? I know just how you feel because I have been there a time or two in my life. Imagine how Lazarus felt. He had a personal relationship with Jesus, yet he lay on a bed of affliction suffering and dying. The relationship that Lazarus had with Jesus should help us to understand that no matter how strong your relationship is, YOU ARE NOT EXCLUDED FROM CIRCUM-STANCES.

We will all suffer and endure trials and tribulations; however, no matter the circumstances, rest assured that Jesus can help you overcome them all. Why? Because He has a personal relationship with you that guarantees that: He will show up, even when others think that there is no hope or that it's too late for you.

Through Jesus Christ, you and I can overcome overwhelming circumstances and PREVAIL. The challenge is that you have to begin to see yourself as an overcomer through Jesus Christ, who gives you the strength to overcome by the Blood of the Lamb.

So remember as the songwriter says: HE MOVES MOUNTAINS, HE CAUSES WALLS TO FALL!!!

Therefore, let us confess that we are: OVERCOM-ERS!

"And when he thus had spoken, he cried with a loud voice, Lazarus, come forth. And he that was dead came forth, bound hand and foot with graveclothes: and his face was bound about with a napkin. Jesus saith unto them, Loose him, and let him go." John 11:43-44 KJV

CHANGE THE PEOPLE YOU ARE AROUND

Stop lending your ear to fools and stop listening to their rambling nonsense. Why do you permit yourself to be around complainers and negative people who are always coming up with one complaint after another with no valid reason at all? If you allow them to rent space in your head for long then you will start to take on their character. This is why when the nation of Israel would conquer an enemy, God would tell them to kill everything that was in the enemy's camp. The reason that God wanted the enemy completely demolished was because he was protecting his people from being assimilated into the culture, character, and ultimately the idolatrous beliefs of the enemy.

Remember that you become what you hang around, so hanging around a fool or someone who is negative all the time will eventually make you become what? You guessed it right, a fool or a negative person.

So here's the solution, in the words of Pastor Sammie D. Simmons, "Change the people you're around or CHANGE THE PEOPLE YOU'RE AROUND!!!"

"Don't waste your breath on fools, for they will despise the wisest advice." Proverbs 23:9

What did you do to earn it? NOTHING
Do you really deserve it? NO
BUT GOD!!!

None of us has done anything to deserve what has been given in our stead! Although we did wrong, although we broke God's law and sinned, another was punished and died in our place. The reality is that He wasn't convicted by mistake, but He IN-TENTIONALLY intervened on our behalf and stood in the place that you & I deserved to be.

So look back over your life, and I promise that you will see a series of "BUT GOD" moments where time and time again he stood in your place and all you will be able to do is to lift your hands and say, BUT GOD!!

"He himself bore our sins {in his body on the cross, so that we might die to sins and live in righteous-

ness} by his wounds you have been healed." 1 Peter
2:24 NIV

PERFECT VISION
20/20

"And Elisha prayed, and said, Lord, I pray thee, open his eyes, that he may see." 1 Kings 6: 17

Have you ever looked at this passage of scripture and wondered, if he could see the army surrounding them? Why did the Prophet Elisha pray that his eye be opened so that he could see? The amazing thing is that there are many in the church that have sight, yet have no vision.

I can recall, as we were rebuilding the sanctuary, that some made the comment that the building looked like a huge barn. I quickly understood that the person could only see what was before their physical eyes and that they did not possess the ability to see the potential thereof. Once you receive vision, you gain the ability to see things beyond the limitations of your eyes.

In other words, Elisha prayed that the Lord would open the spiritual eyes or the understanding of his servant so that he could see the possibilities of God, instead of the impossibilities of man. This is the prayer of every Pastor or leader of an organization that the people around them would be able to see the possibility of a thing instead of the limitations of what they see before them. The writer of the Gospel of Luke said it best in the first chapter and the thirty-seventh verse, "For with God nothing shall be impossible."

So I pray that in 2020 the Lord will open your eyes so that you may have the vision to see clearer than you've ever seen before. God is executing his plan all around you, even when you cannot see his hand at work. So let us draw closer to him in this season so that He will grant us Perfect Vision to clearly see what's around us.

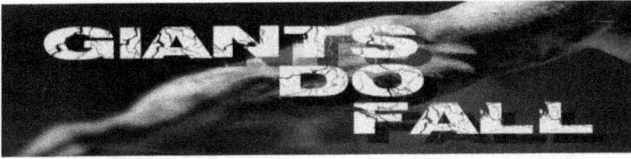

GIANTS DO FALL

Have you ever had a situation seem insurmountable? Have you ever been overwhelmed? Have you ever been in a situation that was so big until you felt getting out was impossible? How did it get so big? The answer is obvious, you made it grow. How? By fearing and worrying about it.

The warriors of Israel were defeated by Goliath because they approached him with fear and trembling instead of with faith. You see, fear will make the things that you are up against seem bigger than what they appear to be, thus making them seem insurmountable, overwhelming, and impossible to overcome.

David did not make the same mistake with Goliath as the others did because David approached him with the right mindset. David spent time alone with God out in the open pasture and realized that the God of the universe has to be bigger than universe that He created. So David stood in awe and worshipped the Lord knowing that with the help of the Lord he had the strength to defeat anything or anybody. So when the lion attacked, David did not respond in fear. When the bear attacked, David did not respond in fear. He responded in faith and his "Giants Fell." Those things that others felt could not be defeated fell at the hands of David.

So what did David do that we often fail to do? He spent time alone in worship and grew his faith bigger than his fear. So when it seemed as if big trouble was before him, his faith, hope, trust, and total reliance upon God grew within, and not his own strength. David responded 1 Samuel 17: 47 *"… for the battle is the LORD's, and he will give you into our hands."*

In other words, David looked at the problem and spoke to it as small, not big. I can hear the voice of Dr. Jasmin Spurlock in my head as I think about David's approach. She said, "GIANTS DO FALL."

So child of God, be encouraged in the midst of what you are going through, speak to it in faith and make your God bigger than that giant of a problem. Always remember when you approach any problem in faith that, 'GIANTS DO FALL.'.

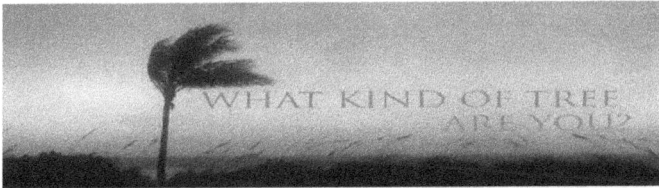

We are all like trees weathering the storms of life; vulnerable, exposed, and effected by our environment in major ways. What were you built for? Will you endure?

Some of us are like Pine trees- they snap easily in the midst one of life's many storms, and they are magnets for lightening; in other words they feed off of drama/trouble.

Some are like Pecan trees- they may get roughed up, beaten and bruised, and some may even snap, but they survive the storm.

Some are like a Palm trees-when the storm comes, they bend, but they don't break. Then after the storm passes by they stand taller than they were before they went through the storm.

A Product of Grace: From the Heart of a Pastor

Some are like the Great Oak Trees-what doesn't kill them only makes them stronger. In other words, they weather the storms of life while seemly growing bigger, better, and stronger as storms pass by.

When the storms of life are raging, and they will rage in your life, it will matter greatly the type of tree that you are. Resiliency, perseverance, strength, and growth are the traits that you will need in order to endure and overcome. I pray that the spirit of the Lord will keep you planted by flowing waters that will nourish and make you stronger.

"And he shall be like a tree planted by the rivers of water, that bringeth forth his fruit in his season; his leaf also shall not wither; and whatsoever he doeth shall prosper." Psalms 1:3 KJV

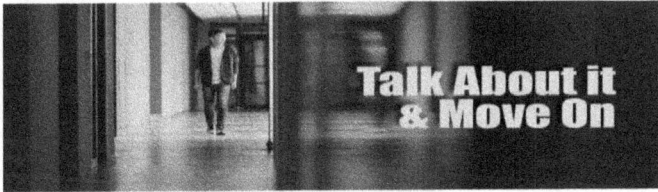

Talk About it & Move On

We grow weary by holding on to old baggage!!! Old baggage is our past issues, past hurt, past pain, past words said by others whom we in turn give lip service to, by saying "I forgive you," yet we still hold on to the memory of the thing because we are scarred!!! The problem with forgiveness intertwined with lip service is that it's superficial. You didn't really mean it, you just said it to save face.

If you truly want to forgive, "TALK ABOUT IT & MOVE ON!!!" After Jacob & his brother met face to face, their past issue was forgotten!!! Never to arise and trouble them any longer! Why? Because they reasoned with each other and came into agreement concerning the past, the present, and the future. In other words, imagine them saying, "OK, that was the past, I was wrong. Please forgive me. How do we move forward from here?"

Let us all learn and value this lesson from Jacob and Esau. STOP holding on to things, JUST LET IT

GO!!! God will not heal what you won't reveal, and He wants to heal you emotionally. So let the Holy Spirit teach you to TALK ABOUT IT AND MOVE ON!

BE FREE!! Today, I declare and decree that I am releasing anything that I hold against any of the Lord's children. Lord, today I am your canvas upon which a picture of emotional freedom may be painted, in Jesus Name AMEN.

"*18 Come now, and let us reason together, saith the Lord: though your sins be as scarlet, they shall be as white as snow; though they be red like crimson, they shall be as wool.*" Isaiah 1:18 KJV

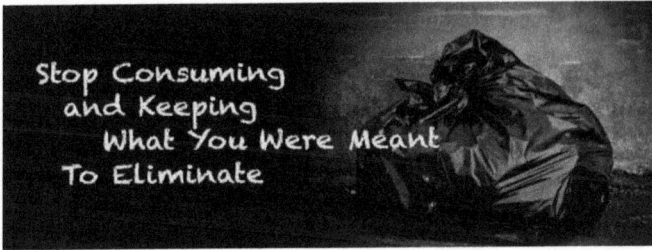

Stop Consuming
and Keeping
What You Were Meant
To Eliminate

Elimination, the act, process, or an instance of discharging, is a natural process. God in His infinite wisdom designed you to be both a consumer and an eliminator. As a consumer, we take in what is necessary to survive and eliminate that which will do us harm. We eat food (consume), absorb the nutrients that are necessary to keep us alive, and eliminate that which will do us harm. Sometimes we get constipation from something that may not agree with our system and this is dangerous because if our body doesn't eliminate the waste it will become toxic and poison us from within

.

Now apply God's simple design to the many relationships that you form during your lifetime. What I mean by that is that we must only keep the relationships that provide the things which are essential to our survival, and eliminate the relationships that will kill us if we hold on to them for too long. All relationships are not meant to nurture and grow you, and some must simply be eliminated in order for you to survive. So after you stop consuming them, all you have remaining to do is to eliminate the toxic relationships that are killing you spiritually if you want to survive the battle that you are in at this moment.

"12 *Wherefore seeing we also are compassed about with so great a cloud of witnesses, let us lay aside (eliminate) every weight, and the sin which doth so easily beset (hinder, destroy) us, and let us run with patience the race that is set before us, 2 Looking unto Jesus the author and finisher of our faith…*" Hebrews 12:1-2

SPEAK THE TRUTH

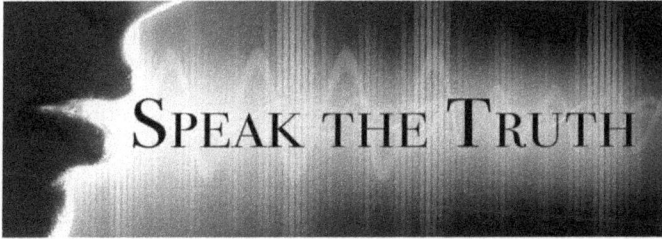

The power of a lie is that it will often cause you to operate in a manner that you usually would not. Most people who are often polite respond with anger when they have been lied upon. In order to overcome the power of a lie, you must resist the temptation to respond when people talk about you. How do you do this? It's simple, STAND ON TRUTH.

Truth is eternal, it pre-existed the lie, and as a matter of fact a lie, comes about when truth is ignored or manipulated. The victory comes from you refusing to be manipulated, ignored, or deceived any longer. The truth shall stand forever but a lie will always fade away. Don't allow lies to come out of your mouth, regardless of what they say, be true to the "Greater" that is within you. You are a vessel of truth because you carry the Holy Spirit and the Word of God within you. Therefore, in response to a lie, only let what's inside of you come out, which is truth!

"For my mouth shall speak truth; and wickedness is an abomination to my lips."
 Proverbs 8:7 KJV

THE GOD
OF
ANOTHER CHANCE

Have you ever heard the statement, "God is a God of a second chance?" Although this is a very popular statement that has been made to be a mantra in the church, this statement is not entirely true. It includes a sprinkling of truth where it states that "God is a God of..." This is a true statement that most of us can conclude with something great that the Lord has done in our lives.

However, we must make it very clear that God is not merely a God of a second chance. If it were so, then upon falling short the second time in any area of the believer's life, we all would be judged to face the consequences of our sin. Therefore, God is NOT a God of a second chance, "God is the God of ANOTHER chance".

The scripture says, "But this I call to mind, and therefore I have hope: The steadfast love of the Lord never ceases; his mercies never come to an end; they are new every morning; great is your faithfulness." Lamentations 3:21-23

With the dawning of a new day, comes God's mercies, or another chance granted by the Lord for us to get it right. Life will present many chances, and many will fall time and time again. But a wise man will always get up and thank God for another chance to get it right, while a fool will simply lie there and waste the gift of the Lord's mercy. Remember every day; all who believe are given another chance to experience the grace and mercy of God. Every day we see that God is merciful towards us, and His mercies will "never come to an end."

Why do you do what you do? Are you doing whatever it is that you were created to do? How confident are you in what it is that you do? Have you ever wondered why you do it?

If you ever searched for the answers to the previous questions, just relax and stay the course. I can imagine in my mind that Jesus may have had these same questions in his life, but he chose to let his PASSION lead him. When you trust God with your life and follow his lead, your passion will lead you before people and to places that you never imagined.

Jesus was known as a carpenter's son who was born in a barn with the animals, yet he refused to let the limitations of life hinder his passion.

It was his passion that pushed him to define his purpose in the temple (Luke 4:17-21). It was his passion at the young age of twelve that pushed him to stay behind and witness the love of God to the elders in the temple (Luke 2:41-52). It was his passion that pushed him to refuse to let the celebration stop as he turned water into wine (John 2:1-11). It was his passion that pushed him into the wilderness to voluntarily be tempted of the devil (Luke 4:1-14). It was his passion that pushed him to declare the goodness of the Lord before thousands of men, women, and children at a time although he was a humble and simple carpenter (Matthew 5:1-11). It was his passion that pushed him to endure the suffering, pain and humiliation of the cross (Matthew 27:32-56). It was his passion that pushed him to offer forgiveness even at the point of death on the cross (Luke 23:24). It was his passion that pushed him into a borrowed tomb (Luke 23:50-53). It was his passion that pushed him to the pit of hell to preach deliverance and lead the captive to freedom in God (1 Peter 3:19). It was his passion that pushed him forth from the grave with all power in his hands (Mark 16:4-6). Finally, it was with and through his passion that he pushed down the power that raised him from the dead and granted it permission to dwell within all of humanity that would receive him as Lord (Ephesians 4:8).

So the question to ponder is: How passionate are you and where will your passion push you?

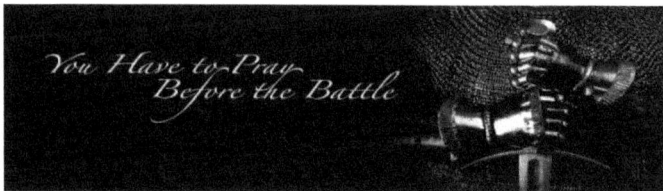

You Have to Pray Before the Battle

Athletes practice, Airmen, Sailors, Soldiers, and Marines all train, Olympians take years getting ready for their Olympic moment, yet most Christians don't do anything to get ready for their moment. Someone once said that, "you either fail to plan or plan to fail." This can hold true in many situations whether physical or spiritual. Jesus introduced us to an amazing concept in his Garden of Gethsemane experience that most of us often overlook, and that is the concept of "PREPARATION."

If you reflect upon the scriptures, Jesus prophesied to his disciples concerning his death several times, yet he continued to work in the field (Jn 9:4). He did not stop and throw a pity party by crying woe is me like we often do. He persevered because he spent time preparing before the battle came. No General would send his troops to engage in battle without proper preparation.

For the believer, we prepare in our secret place talking to God through prayer. It is in prayer (commuication with God) where the believer receives clear instruction, guidance, and is strengthened in the inner man through the person of the Holy Spirit. A believer will fall short and ultimately fail if he/she hasn't spent time preparing before engaging. Jesus gave us the perfect example of the power of preparation through prayer as he spent time in prayer in the Garden of Gethsemane (Lk 22:39-44) speaking to the Father before engaging in the greatest battle of His life. So, let us remember to spend time praying so that when the battle comes, we can, Stand still and see the salvation of the Lord for this battle is not yours, it is the Lord's.

Here's an amazing fact about your church that may be as a surprise to you. Not everyone in the church has the same purpose for being there. Some are placed there to be uplifting, supportive, and encouraging (Wheat), while some are there merely to wreak havoc, be negative, and to sow discord while trying to undermine the vision of the house (Tare). Once we realize that we have two types of people in the church, we place the unrealistic expectation upon the pastor to divide and conquer.

Here's a newsflash, stop expecting the pastor to isolate and eliminate the wheat from the tare, it's not the pastor's responsibility. The pastor's responsibility is to feed and nurture the wheat and the tare the same. Yes, both the wheat and the tare consume and grow from the same food, drink the same water, and intake the same light, but their purpose and intent are different. One gives life (wheat) and the other tries to destroy (tare) the life of the giver.

Our assignment as wheat is to love the tare and to let them grow side by side with us until Christ himself divides and set asunder. Yes, worship next to them, and show them the love of Christ in you, all the while praying that repentance will come unto them before it's too late.

Jesus clearly discussed this in *"The Parable of the Wheat and the Tares,"* found in Matthew 13:24-30 where it is written as follows:

[24] *Another parable He put forth to them, saying: "The kingdom of heaven is like a man who sowed good seed in his field;* [25] *but while men slept, his enemy came and sowed tares among the wheat and went his way.* [26] *But when the grain had sprouted and produced a crop, then the tares also appeared.* [27] *So the servants of the owner came and said to him, 'Sir, did you not sow good seed in your field? How then does it have tares?'* [28] *He said to them, 'An enemy has done this.' The servants said to him, 'Do you want us then to go and gather them up?'* [29] *But he said, 'No, lest while you gather up the tares you also uproot the wheat with them.* [30] *Let*

both grow together until the harvest, and at the time of harvest I will say to the reapers, "First gather together the tares and bind them in bundles to burn them, but gather the wheat into my barn."'

Are you Wheat or Tare? EVERY CHURCH HAS BOTH, WHICH ONE ARE YOU?

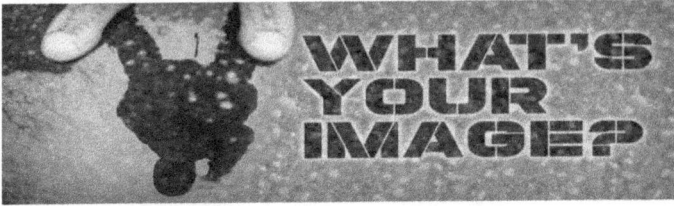

There's two ways to see yourself: through the eyes of others or through a mirror. We were created in the image and likeness of the triune Godhead.

Therefore, what we project should look like God. What people should see when they see you is (1) "love, joy, peace, longsuffering, gentleness, goodness, faith, Meekness, temperance (Galatians 5:22)."

However, there are some who claim to know God, yet they often reflect (2) *"haughty eyes, a lying tongue, hands that shed innocent blood, a heart that devises wicked schemes, feet that are quick to rush into evil, false witness who pours out lies, and a person who stirs up conflict in the community."* Proverbs 6:16-19 NIV

The first eight things will make you reflect the image of God, while the latter seven will cause you to reflect or project what God hates.

So, what do you reflect or project? What's your image? What do others see in you?

Be sure that your image reflects the love of God and draws others to Him instead of pushing them away. Think about it, others are watching you, and what they see matters. What's your image?

Surprise, you are in control of your own reward. You can't be voted off the island, you can't be evicted from the house, and you can't be fired, BUT you can be condemned to eternal fire if you don't stick to the plan!!!

King Saul was given simple instructions by God, and because he chose not to follow them, he lost both his kingdom and his life! What price are you willing to pay for your arrogance, for your stubbornness, or for simply ignoring God's plan for your life? You can't have it your way, it's God's way or no way at all. Are you willing to lose it all with one choice? My brothers and sister, I hope not. Don't die spiritually because you're singing, "I did it my way!" Look how far doing it your way has gotten you!

TODAY YOU HAVE TO CHOOSE!!!

SO, WHAT SHALL IT BE?

CHOOSE WISELY!

MOST IMPORTANTLY, CHOOSE GOD'S PLAN!!

"And *if it seem evil unto you to serve the LORD, choose you this day whom ye will serve; whether the gods which your fathers served that were on the other side of the flood, or the gods of the Amorites, in whose land ye dwell: but as for me and my house, we will serve the LORD*." Joshua 24:15 KJV

Isn't it amazing that in the midst of a pandemic where mankind is on a level playing field that more people are still drawn to the world than to the church? Has our testimony become so watered down? Has our salt lost its flavor until the church is now irrelevant?

No, it is simply because even in the midst of perilous times, mankind is still drawn to satisfy the lusts of the flesh. On tonight, I saw two live feeds on Facebook. One had 6.7 thousand viewers while the other had 45. One was of a bible study and the other was a local disc jockey playing club music; which one drew the largest crowd? Yes, you guessed correct, it was the DJ playing music.

I found it amazing that people were more lifted by the music than by the gospel. Has the salt lost its flavor? What did Jesus mean when he said, *"You are the salt of the earth?"* But if the salt loses its *saltiness, how can it be made salty again? It is no longer good for anything, except to be thrown out and trampled underfoot.*" (Matt. 5:13 NIV)

The salt in those days was unprocessed and unrefined like the table salt that we have today. In other words, at best, it was a poor-quality rock salt. Salt in the region around Israel came from the rock salt found by the Dead Sea. It was hastily and crudely gathered. This meant that dirt and other impurities were collected with it into the bag. If the salt got wet it dissolved and the insoluble bits of rock would remain. Because the air in the region around Israel was so dry, it didn't take much moisture to dissolve the salt and leave behind a bag of useless tiny stones. Once this happened, the salt content was lost and it was no longer useful. The best place for the user to get rid of the salt was to dispose of in the street, where it was "trampled underfoot" by pedestrians.

We who have received salvation through our Lord and Savior Jesus Christ must ensure that we remain true to God's word and that our witness remains strong. This is necessary in order to ensure that the church remains relevant, especially to a world who has found itself in crisis. In times like these if we remain faithful and strong in our faith, then we will lead the world to the only solution, the only healing; which lies in Christ and Christ alone.

Remember you have not lost your flavor, meaning that your witness should change everything that it comes in contact with. So, my brothers and my sisters, stay salty and change the world.

SHAKE IT OFF!

Don't spend your time wallowing in sorrow. Don't spend your time shedding tears! When they ignore you, ostracize you, push you aside, and knock you down, GET UP & KEEP MOVING FORWARD!!!

My brothers and my sisters, be sure to check your relationships and be sure that we never give any man or woman so much power over you until you feel like you can't live without them. The only one that you can't live without is JESUS!! So, when they push you away, DON'T FRET & DON'T FALL APART, shake the dust off your feet and let God handle it.

You can't afford to allow your emotions to get the best of you. SHAKE IT OFF! God has always provided you a way of escape. How? By putting more trust in Him than you put in them. Be encouraged my brothers and sisters.

"And whosoever shall not receive you, nor hear your words, when ye depart out of that house or city, shake off the dust of your feet." Matthew 1014 KJV

TURN OFF THE NOISE!

Have you looked around for the last few weeks long enough to take note of what is going on? As social distancing takes effect and towns, states, and nations around the world are locking down, something unique is happening. The hands of time and nature seem to be moving in reverse, the air is cleaner, the lakes are clearer, the wind seems to blow constantly and for the first time in a long time, it is as if all of nature is singing. Why is this happening? Because the noise has stopped and the presence of God walks upon the earth in the cool of the day once more. The time has arrived for us to remain silent and wait for the Lord to speak once more.

People, places, and things around the world have been silenced in the midst of this pandemic and we who believe in God are sensing and seeing His move throughout the land. Now that the noise is off all of creation is crying out for God and He is responding now more than ever.

Now that the noise has been silenced you are in a season of asking, hearing, and manifestation.

What does that mean? It means that whatever you ask of God in faith He will hear you and shall bring it to pass. So let us not grow weary in the midst of silence, God is about to bless you in the midst of a desolate place. Now that you've turned off the noise get ready to hear Him speak clearer than you've ever heard him before. Your season has arrived and the greater glory of the Lord is upon you.

"20 *But the LORD is in his holy temple: let all the earth keep silence before him.*" Habakkuk 2:20

Don't you realize that you can't tell everybody everything? The fact of the matter is that sometimes your mouth will get you in trouble if your mouth is bigger than your anointing. Some people that you know, or that simply hang around you are spiritually incompetent. Which means that they simply are not capable of handling everything that God shows you, so be careful who you share your vision with. However, even when we falter and talk too much, God makes it work for our good.

Joseph shared his vision with his brothers who couldn't handle it, and jealousy caused them to betray him and throw him into the pit. Who have you been talking to that's been pushing you in the pit? There are two types of people that are hearing your vision; they are pit people and palace people. The problem is that most of us only meet our palace people after dealing with our pit people.

If Joseph hadn't been pushed by the pit people he would never been in prison and met the one who pushed him to the palace. So, even when we run our mouths too much, keep trusting God and he will push you into the presence of palace people through your pit.

"As for you, you meant evil against me, but God meant it for good, to bring it about that many people should be kept alive, as they are today." Genesis 50:20 ESV

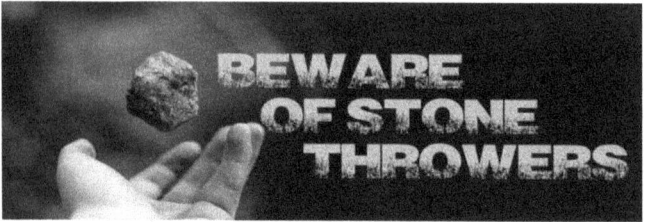

Have you ever known anyone who's always toting news, good or bad? They run back and forth sowing discord, always challenging your credibility? They always begin the conversation with, "can you believe that so and so did or said." Then, after they have unloaded all of their discord on you, the next thing they are going to say is, "what you think about that?" Their objective is simply to get you to talk about someone or something, or simply to pull you into their mess so that they can accuse you of wrong doing. BEWARE, these people are stone throwers, and they have baited the trap that will allow them to stone you to death. This is the very same tactic that they used on Jesus in John 8:1-8.

They came to him with the intent to entrap him into either violating Roman law or violating the Law of Moses to discredit him. However, we have to do as Jesus did; 1) be slow to speak, 2) let them reveal the intent of their heart, 3) use Godly wisdom to turn their traps back on them, and 4) watch them drop their stones and walk away. Although they have stones and the intent to destroy you, be encouraged by the words found in the Book of Isaiah 54:17,

"No weapon that is formed against thee shall prosper; and every tongue that shall rise against thee in judgment thou shalt condemn. This is the heritage of the servants of the LORD, and their righteousness is of me, saith the LORD." The weapons, the stones, will form against you, but they shall not prosper. BEWARE of Stone throwers.

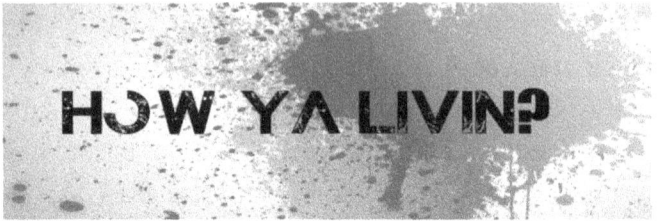

HOW YA LIVIN?

Have you ever heard the question posed, "How ya livin?" In some regions this used to be a popular way to greet one another. I wonder what response we would receive if we started greeting one another this way in churches across the world, and require an honest response?

If we would really be honest, here are some of the responses that you would hear from those who confess that they know Christ:

- I lie too much
- I drink too much
- I cheat on my spouse
- I'm sexually immoral
- I live an alternative lifestyle
- And here's an oldie but goodie, "I'm just a sinner saved by grace!!!"

The problem is that it is impossible to live what we fail to confess. So the next time someone asks you, "How ya livin?" Simply say to them and to your-selves, "I am Holy, I am the righteousness of God in Christ Jesus."

For the Scripture says concerning you in,
1 Peter 1: 15-16
"But as he which hath called you is holy, so be ye holy in all manner of conversation; Because it is written, Be ye holy; for I am holy.
2 Corinthians 5:21
"For he hath made him to be sin for us, who knew no sin; that we might be made the righteousness of God   in   him."

So when you know who you are, it's easy to con-fess, "How ya livin!"

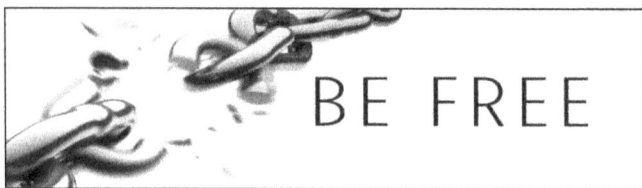

BE FREE

I have exciting news! If you are reading this message, it means that the Lord has kept you, and you survived every attack and overcame every obstacle that was placed in your pathway. Think about how many times your faith was challenged in the last 365 days, think about how many times you felt like giving up and walking away, and think about how many times you may have felt like you were bound.

Every obstacle that the enemy sent your way was designed to challenge your faith and cause you to believe his lies. Why? Because he knows that if he causes you to believe his lies then it will create a chasm between you and God. Not a literal separation of earth, but a spiritual separation from God and His will for your life. A spiritual chasm is a profound difference between people, viewpoints, feelings, etc... The enemy wants to create a profound difference between what God says and what you believe, and to accomplish this he uses lies to keep the believer bound.

To combat the enemy's deception and lies, our Heavenly Father sent "TRUTH" into the world to provide us an example of how we can walk in truth and resist personal destruction.

Remember, Jesus Christ came to set you free. Free from the lies and the deception of the enemy that causes us to fall short of what God has ordained for our lives.

The Scripture says in John 8:32 NIV *"And ye shall know the truth, and the truth shall make you free."* What enables Jesus Christ (the TRUTH) of God to make you free? The fact is that the TRUTH died to pay the debt of the bondage of lies and deception and arose so that you and I could be made free in him.

So REFUSE TO BE BOUND any longer, accept or come to know the TRUTH (Jesus), and BE FREE!

An Attitude
of Gratitude

There are a lot of people out there walking around with the wrong attitude concerning life. Most take life for granted and expect that they simply deserve everything that they have. Some even feel that they are self-made and earned everything by themselves or on their own.

However, there is nothing that neither you nor I have done to deserve all of the many blessings that the Lord has afforded us to have. It is merely a result of God's unmerited favor towards us. What do I mean? First of all, it was God's desire that you were even born. It was God that kept you alive through the many risks that you took with a life that wasn't even your own. It was God's Grace that saved you from the debt of sin. It was God's good pleasure for you to prosper and be in good health.

If for no other reason at all, it's good manners to say "Thank You" to anyone who does anything for you. However, since God has done it all, the least we can do is walk around with an attitude of gratitude and "THANK HIM."

So look back over your life and say, 'THANK YOU LORD FOR ALL YOU HAVE DONE FOR ME."

"in everything give thanks; for this is the will of God in Christ Jesus for you." 1 Thessalonians 5:18 NKJ

The journey that has been set before you may be long, exhausting, and even difficult, but God created you and only you for this journey. He has already given you all that you need to make it to an expected end.

Joseph's journey was difficult, but God showed him flashes of the promise even before his journey began. Remember the flashes that God has already shown you and be quickened in your spirit because He has STRENGTHENED you for what lies ahead. At every difficult time in Joseph's life, the scripture states, "And the Lord was with Joseph," remember Christ promised never to leave you nor to forsake you. Be encouraged my brother, and my sister, the Lord will never send you on a journey that he won't walk beside you on while you're traveling.

So be STRONG in the Lord and in the power of his might and endure this journey like a good soldier, because you have the strength to survive. Now go forth in the strength of the Lord.

"I will go in the strength of the Lord GOD..."
~Psalm 71:6

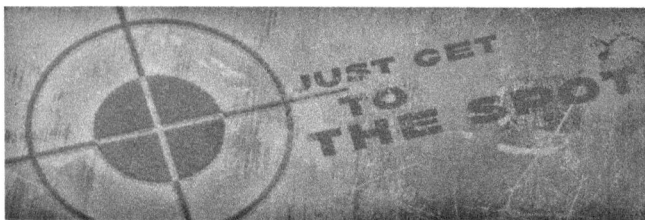

You are not a mistake! You are here for a purpose that's greater than you can ever imagine, but the enemy desires to distract you from your purpose by blocking your path with his schemes. Why? Because he understands that if you ever get to your spot, then the greater within you shall rise.

What spot? The place or location along this journey called life that God has preordained, predetermined, and predestined to meet you at to empower you for what lies ahead. Saul had no idea that his spot was on the Damascus road, but when he reached his spot, Jesus was already standing there. Immediately Saul's forward progress to do evil stopped, and the Lord redirected his path and transformed his life to do good.

Now the Lord wants to do the same thing for you, but you have to refuse to be distracted or denied and just get to the spot. Remember that Jesus is standing there waiting and He's about to transform your life for the good.

"For I am persuaded, that neither death, nor life, nor angels, nor principalities, nor powers, nor things present, nor things to come, nor height, nor depth, nor any other creature, shall be able to separate us from the love of God, which is in Christ Jesus our Lord." ~ Romans 8:38-39

About the Author

Walter Robertson, III, epitomizes the scripture "Many are called but few are Chosen." He is a Pastor and School Counselor, with a passion for and a genuine love for all children of God. Pastor Robertson is a devoted vessel of God, whom was chosen by God to preach the Gospel. He believes that we all need to be encouraged and lifted up occasionally, particularly during the tough times in our lives. He has dedicated his life and ministry to uplifting people as his mission is "to call people's lives back to order." Pastor Robertson serves as the senior pastor of Union Baptist Church of Rembert, SC, Inc. This fast-growing ministry is thriving spiritually under his leadership. He believes in the power of words as he speaks with wisdom, knowledge, and truth. Pastor Robertson recognizes that sharing the right words, to the right person, at the right moment in time can change their life forever. His ability to lead from the forefront allows him to be an example to others with a gift to effectively communicate with the youth that he encounters. He is passionate about education and strives to be an example for younger generations; as he inspires them to realize that they are capable of being successful and encourages them to take advantage of the opportunities that the Lord puts before them. This vibrant man of God is no stranger to his community and continues to pour back in to the places where his feet tread. For booking speaking engagements you may contact Pastor Robertson via email at Rev.walterrobertson@gmail.com.

About the Graphic Designer

Dionya Kelley, owner of Dionya Designs, a graphic design company specializing in visual brand identity and graphic design, is a native and resident of Charlotte, North Carolina. She has over 20 years of graphic design experience, and has made appearances at various conferences as a keynote speaker encouraging others to invest in proper branding and digital communications. Graphic Design is her career, but building the Kingdom of God is what Dionya Kelley aspires to do every day. She has served in various capacities to this aim as a preacher of the Gospel in the pulpit, a guest speaker and minister to the youth at youth conferences, and a keynote speaker to small ministry groups. She is also the coordinator of digital communications at her home church in Fort Mill, South Carolina. Dionya Kelley is a wife and a mother of 2 boys, all who keep her balanced, grounded, and encouraged. Dionya Kelley has the heart and passion to help others grow and it shows. Her peers and those whom she serve often call her "smiley" and "sunshine"!

A Product of Grace: From the Heart of a Pastor

PTP

Pure Thoughts Publishing LLC

www.ingramcontent.com/pod-product-compliance
Lightning Source LLC
LaVergne TN
LVHW041206080426
835508LV00008B/822